EternalE

[Definition]
G & J Entertainment LLC 2016

[def-uh-nish-uh n]

Acknowledgements

For Mom, Dad, Meredith,
Coleman, Rachel, Dustin, Stephanie,
Ana, Adalyn, Simeon,
Alex, John F., Haymaker & Ki-Ki,
Kimberly, Shelby, Jacob,
Clarice Pollock & John H. Pollock Sr.
Helen Geraci & Charles Geraci
The Pollock Family & The Geraci Family
Louisville, KY & Clarksville, TN
This book is also dedicated to the memory of
John H. Pollock Jr.
"Keep doing what you're doing,
cause you're doing it well." - Uncle John

-Outlaw G

For Mom, Dad
Tim & Noah
Thank you to the reader for giving us your time
and your engagement.

-Alex

[def-uh-nish-uh n]

EternalE

- The Bottom
- Time Never Wasted
- Why Are You So Messy?
- One Day
- Fear Is
- Liar
- The Woman In Chains
- The Bound Man
- The Forgotten Child
- Love Is
- Love's Lesson
- EternalE

[def-uh-nish-uh n]

The Bottom

Fear has the ability to hinder even the most courageous people. It is when we allow fear to consume us, we fall to the bottom of a pit. We fear that we are incapable of climbing out of this dark hole. Due to our lack of love and understanding, we remain trapped. It is until we decide to let love be our guide, our path to climb remains clouded. When we choose fear, we remain stagnant in our ways. When we choose love, we begin our ascension from darkness…

-Outlaw G

[def-uh-nish-uh n]

The Bottom

Fear…
It will always try to hold you down.
Open your eyes and see how
Your life looks,
Right now…
You may feel as if
You are trapped at the bottom of a pit,
Fear makes your heart shift
When you think about the life you've missed,
You're left with only one wish…

To get out…

Heart broken
Body broken
Feeling as if you are at the bottom,
As if your soul was stolen.
Breathe life in with these words,
Understand and know this.

Everybody hurts
You will not be the last
And you are not the first.
As of right now you are hurt
You are dying of thirst,
Every gift you receive
You believe
Will become a curse.
Being alone makes you feel worse
Trapped with a diminished spirit,
Your soul is crying out now
Praying someone will hear it.

[def-uh-nish-uh n]

Fear…

It is fear that has clouded your mind
It is fear that damages your heart,
It is here and now you begin to understand
Love is where your climb will start.

Reach out with your hands to grasp,
To the soil that has left you trapped.
Ring out with your voice to be heard,
Your ascension begins with one word.

Love…

One word
Four letters of choice,

One speaks volumes
The other silences your voice.

You may be down now
But you can climb out,
It is here you must not fear
So your love can be found…

Rise out of that dark
Love won't let you be forgotten,
Let love be your start…

[def-uh-nish-uh n]

Or let fear keep you at the bottom.

[def-uh-nish-uh n]

Time Never Wasted

Life can sometimes break us down. It may feel at times that we are, in a way, wasting it. It is fear and depression that can creep in and makes us feel unfulfilled during these times. What one should remember, is that time spent with love, is time that is never wasted. Time with your spouse, friends, or time alone, is never wasted when it is done through love. Your life is not a waste and you are not a waste of life. Live with love, thus your time will never be wasted.

-Outlaw G

Time Never Wasted

At times
Fear makes us selfish,
Trapped inside our own minds
Isolation renders us helpless.
Love is selfless
It does not dwell in inequity,
But when love is false, all pay the cost
This is forgotten too easily…

You cannot be everything to everyone
This is just not logical,
But each of us can be something to someone
Through love all things are possible.
When you truly love someone
You love them most of all,
With a grip that will never let them slip
You will never let them fall.
Because love will never break you
It will never leave you hurt,
True love,
Is above all else,
If you truly know its worth…

It can be a struggle
One to push the other to pull,
Sometimes love can make you crazy
It can make you act like a fool.
Love is swift
Love is thick
It can never ever be see-through,
Real love is due love,
It will always be true.

[def-uh-nish-uh n]

True to who?
True to you
With anyone you share,
Love is everlasting
Love is ever grasping
Love is never gasping
Like being short of air.
Love fears nothing
It will be always there,
Love is simple
So very simple,
As telling someone you care.
Love endures
It is an unbreakable force,
That can never be splintered, shattered
Or thrown off course.
Love is clarity,
To some this is a rarity,
For love achieves for the mind,
Body, and soul
To be free.

Love is a word that comes from the spirit
It doesn't always have to be said for you to hear it,
You should never fear it
Instead embrace it,
For love is constant
No being
No thought
Nothing,
Could ever erase it.
When love finds you
Don't be shy, face it,
Take your time
For time used with love,

Is time never wasted…

[def-uh-nish-uh n]

Love can only grow
It gains strength from within,
It is a feeling that grants healing
No matter what situation you're in.
Love will never leave you lost
It will never lead you astray,
For true love is the light
On any darkened pathway.
Even on your darkest days
When life seems so grim,
Keep love on your side
Let love be your time
And know that love never ends.

[def-uh-nish-uh n]

<u>Why Are You So Messy?</u>

We all have encountered someone in our lives who is intolerable. Those individuals blame their problems on others, never taking responsibility for their actions, and continuously gossip for the sake of their own entertainment. Being "messy" is very prevalent in people who fear what they are, and/or fear what they cannot be. Those that are messy generally do not love themselves, instead, they project their fear (of who or what they are) on others. Are you messy? If so, why? It is never to late to clean up your mess…

-Outlaw G

[def-uh-nish-uh n]

Why Are You So Messy?

You claim you know love
But instead you throw shade,
It is all because
Of this mess that you've made...

But Why Are You So Messy?

Every time you open your mouth
Your voice, when I hear it
It seems to be full of doubt,
Because you don't really know what you're talking about,
Only misinformation seems to come out...

So Why Are You So Messy?

(For the messy ladies)
You lie and you cheat
You stay on repeat
Never thinking before you speak,
Separates the strong from the weak…
Your loose lips sinks ships
I'm talking about both pairs,
You never think of the consequences
You become a burden to bear…

But Why Are You So Messy?

(For the messy fellas)
You claim you know knowledge
You claim you know wisdom
But instead you show ignorance
In almost every instance,

[def-uh-nish-uh n]

You can't see your mess
But I see it from a distance,
That's why I'm over here
And you're over there
So let's talk about the difference…
That's why I'm over here screaming to you,

WHY ARE YOU SO MESSY?!

You can't comprehend
This mess that you're in,
Its so bad it's on your soul
It will never be cleansed,
I won't consider you close
I don't consider you friend,
Which means all you have is your mess
That's all you have in the end…

But Why Are You So Messy?

Look at this mess that you've made
With all of these games that you've played,
But maybe it was the game that played you
That makes us all want to say...

Why… Are… You… So… Messy?

It's your mess
It's your stress
Now you gotta be in it,
It's your bed
Where you lay your head
Now you gotta sleep in it.
You crossed too many lines
Told too many lies
Got caught up in the mess,
Now you want to break down and cry.

[def-uh-nish-uh n]

You want to whine and complain
And tell everyone your pain
But when it's all said and done,
You will still have to explain…

Why Are You So Messy?

Well…
You truly are a blessing
A messy blessing in disguise,
Because you allow the world to see your mess,
It is something you can't hide.
Because you alone yourself,
Are the cause of your demise,
It is this mess.
It is your mess.
That has taken over your life...

This is why

You

Are

So

Messy.

[def-uh-nish-uh n]

<u>One Day</u>

It is my belief that we all encounter days where we do not love ourselves. Our lives and the world around us may feel like they are crashing down, pushing us to our mental and emotional limits. "One Day" is a reminder that you will face these hardships, but you **<u>will</u>** persevere through them. It is love for yourself that will lead to love from others. Let love be what gets you through your days so that "One Day", you will be at peace with yourself, and the world around you.

-Outlaw G

[def-uh-nish-uh n]

One Day

One Day.

You will wake up and not be
So blind to the world
That you cannot see,
So closed off from what you cannot be.

One Day.

You will walk without pain
Of the weight of the world weighing on your brain,
No longer will you wear a badge of shame
That you constantly see a blemish or a stain.

One Day.

You will see your own face
And never allow fear to ever displace
How you feel about yourself
You will love what you used to hate.

One Day.

The world will love you
As you have loved
For it is your love that creates love because,
It creates a bond never broken
From a word forever spoken,
Your mind has now awoken
Your soul could never be stolen,
Your heart could never be frozen
It is forever holding,

[def-uh-nish-uh n]

Joy without pain
Light without rain,
To ignite the eternal flame

One Life.

One Day.

[def-uh-nish-uh n]

<u>Fear Is</u>

The opposite of love is not hate, it is Fear.
It is my belief that Fear is the driving factor
behind the majority of the world's
problems. The lack of understanding is
what drives people to lash out in anger, it is
the fear that creates this lack of
understanding. The absence of love is that
fear that consumes the hearts and minds of
those that chose to do ill to their fellow
being. Fear is a wedge to keep us from
each other.

-Outlaw G

Fear Is

Fear is what darkens the skies above
Not allowing you to see the light of Love,
Fear clouds the mind
Fear confuses your thoughts,
Fear makes you hurt
Not knowing the time you've lost.

Fear is…

Fear is the argument you have
With friends or family members when you are mad,
Over things that are so easily fixed
Fear is what provides poison to the mix.
Fear blinds the eyes that have the sight of precision
Fear deafens the ears of understanding to listen,
For fear is the culprit of all indecision
It thrives on the lives that lack definition.

Fear is…

Fear is what stops progress
Instead,
Fear makes us regress
Into something less,
Of what we are supposed to be
Fear is a locked cage that has a lost key.
For fear can make you feel trapped behind bars,
Leaving you with mental,
Physical,
And emotional scars.
Anger and hate both play their part,
It is fear that generates these emotions from the very start.

[def-uh-nish-uh n]

Fear is the lack of understanding
The inability to listen,
No room for compromise
Fear takes its position of infliction.
Fear separates
Fear deviates
To keep us from each other,
Disrespect for your mother
Running a foul to your brother,
Not honoring your father,
Not protecting your daughter,
Fear makes it clear,
Fear makes love a bother…
Fear is the payment
For love that isn't free.
For Fear is
What love could never be.

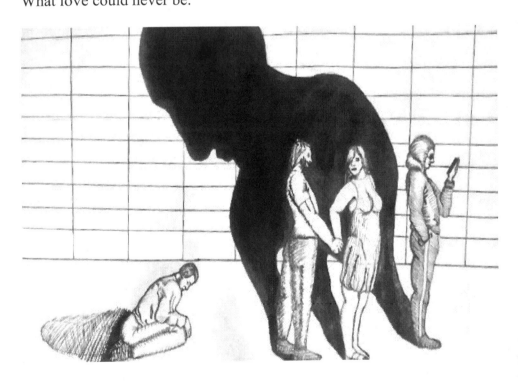

Fear…   Is…   Not…

[def-uh-nish-uh n]

<u>Liar</u>

Fear can turn any honest person into a liar. When it comes to relationships, it is fear that generally creates the most friction and causes the most problems. When one continuously lies, they are consumed with fear that they will no longer be able to control their partner. It is fear that drives the liar to maintain the facade that love is present. Fear is the liar's best tool in controlling their partner. Be wary of those who aim to use fear as a tool against you in any of your relationships.

-Outlaw G

Liar

You lied to me.

You said you would always be there
You said you were here because you cared
You said this life was our burden to bear
But fear wouldn't let love be fair,

So you lied to me…

You said I'd never shed a tear
You said I had nothing to fear
But the fear of nothing became something
Now nothing is what appears,

Because you lied to me…

You said you would be by my side
In this world and this life,
But when I look into your eyes
I see past your disguise.
With every breath that you take
I realize it was fake,
This home that we made
It was made up,
Played up,
Which means I made a mistake.
You have love in your heart,
Is that what you claim?
That too was a lie
And I have you to blame,

Because you lied to me…

[def-uh-nish-uh n]

I am no angel
But I had no angle,
I was trying to give you my world
But even that was painful.
You took my words and twisted
Everything I shared with you was gifted
But instead you try to flip it
To leave my heart wounded and inflicted.
So love shifted,
To no love
But worst of all
I lost love for myself,
I lost who I was.
You let the lies consume your life
Your lies are now your truth,
There is nothing left to say
There is nothing left to do,
It is all because of you.

You lied to me…

[def-uh-nish-uh n]

The Woman in Chains

It is my belief that most women are held back from thriving in life due to society itself. Abusive partners, lack of self confidence due to societal pressures, lack of advancement due to systemic sexism, all are links in the chains that weigh women down. This piece is to bring light to women's plight, but to also share some hope for those that may feel that they are being weighted down by the chains… You have the strength to remove them.

-Outlaw G

[def-uh-nish-uh n]

The Woman in Chains

The Woman in Chains,
Is held back by the abuse of another
Held back by the abuse of a lover
It is this abuse that will take her under
If you could see what the abuse has done to her,
She is held back by the chains of her heart.

The Woman in Chains,
Is controlled by fear
Controlled by her tears
Not seen by her peers
But still they appear,
She is controlled by the chains of her mind.

The Woman in Chains,
Is constricted by a system
It constricts her to be a victim
Weighted down by these chains
She can never lift them,
She is weighted down by the chains of her soul.

The Woman in Chains,
She has been stuck for an eternity
Waiting to break free
For the world to see
She is more than what you want her to be,
She is more.
A woman with pain
A woman with stains
Of blood, sweat, and time,
Her tears like rain,
She was left behind.

[def-uh-nish-uh n]

For her shackles have yet to be broken,
These chains were put on her,
These chains were not chosen.

Something has awoken
Deep inside
Of this Woman in Chains
Something has come alive.

To break these chains of the mind, soul, and heart,
To break these chains and begin a fresh start.

These chains cannot contain the strength she posses,
They will not be her grave
They will not put her to rest.

Break out of these chains, set yourself free,
Break out of these chains so you will no longer be,
The Woman in Chains.

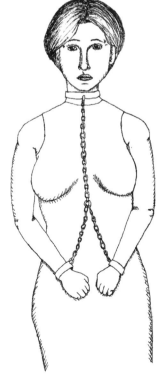

Break Free...

[def-uh-nish-uh n]

The Bound Man

It is my belief that men are bound by societal norms and societal pressures. "Act like a man," "Only girls cry," "Suck it up," all are disparaging and hurtful phrases thrown around in describing how men should "act". Men put so much pressure on themselves to do well in life, if one comes up short, he is labeled a failure. Men must never show their vulnerable side in any instance, no tears, no emotions, all based on what "society" deems fit. "The Bound Man" describes how these societal norms arc damaging to the psyche of men… But also that men do have the strength and the ability to break free of these binds and be who they choose to be, not who society wants them to be.

-Outlaw G

[def-uh-nish-uh n]

The Bound Man

The Bound Man,
Is held back by the lack of understanding
That he as a man can no longer stand the
Pressures of life
To be more than he can
If he doesn't succeed
He is labeled less than
A man
Because this world
Doesn't understand,
His heart…

The Bound Man,
Is ruled by the fear
That if he were to ever shed a tear
It appears
His peers
Will cast him down
Thus leaving him bound,
By the ropes that bind his mind…

The Bound Man,
Is controlled by a system
That states that he can never be a victim
But his hands are tied behind his back
Leaving him open for attack
He cannot defend
From the position he is in
He will not win
For being him… Is a "SIN"
He is bound by the conflict in his soul…

[def-uh-nish-uh n]

The Bound Man,
He is bound waiting to be released
So that he can find his own peace
Within himself he will not rest until,
He finds the understanding that evades him still.
The knot holding his hands
Are the plans of others that restrain this man
To keep him from who he is supposed to be.

He must break free.

So the world can see,

That he is more
Like the woman in chains before
He is more than what you want him to be.

Society will hurt him
Try to break him
Try to make him into what it sees fit
But he will not stand for it,
Nor will he bow to it.

He will break these binds of the mind, heart, and soul
He will no longer be left out in the cold
He will find the woman that was left in chains
To remove his own and to quell her pain,
For the rain falls on them both
Both are just the same.

When they join together
The rain dissipates
The pain alleviates
Their love mediates
For he will no longer be,
Bound to society and its strictly laid plans,
No longer will he be,

[def-uh-nish-uh n]

The Bound Man.

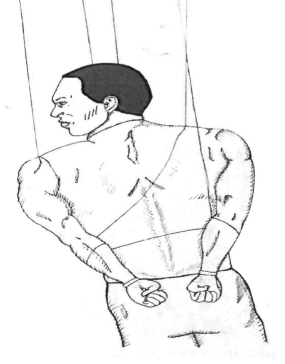

[def-uh-nish-uh n]

The Forgotten Child

It is my belief that society creates "Forgotten Children" every day. It is not the fault of the mother ("The Woman In Chains"), nor the father ("The Bound Man"), for society has created them as well. It is these "Forgotten Children" that have to face the world alone due to the binds of their parents, thus creating more "Women in Chains" and "Bound Men" as offspring. It is up to us as a society to stop this cycle of creating "Forgotten Children". It is through love and understanding that this is achicvable. Find "The Forgotten Child" and free them of their own bonds.

-Outlaw G

[def-uh-nish-uh n]

The Forgotten Child

The Forgotten Child,
Is held back and abandoned
For the life that was granted
Has left the child stranded
Confused and abused.
The child is without Love…
Life…
Or hope…
The child is granted none,
The world has taken this child's heart…

The Forgotten Child,
Sheds the most tears
Has the most fears
For the parents do not appear
To love
To show love
To know love
There is no love to hold the child up
The world has taken this child's mind…

The Forgotten Child,
Is the victim of the system
Victimized by the lies inflicted
Left behind, a life wasted?
No, but still faced with,
No guidance, no path.

Like the father left open for attack
Like the mother weighted down by chains
The child is bound by pain,
The world has taken this child's soul…

[def-uh-nish-uh n]

The Forgotten Chid,
Is left behind
Waiting to be saved
From the life that was given
So that life can be changed
Because at a young age
The child was shattered
Broken because this life did not matter.
No love, no laughter
No symbol of hope
No one to run to
No hands to hold.

No.

No more.

No more will the world be cold
No longer will the child wander
Alone on this road,
For the child will find
That in these dark times
One finds themself
One finds their life.

Even though this child was left behind,
The world will not leave the child undefined.
The child will rewind
Remove the chains
Remove the binds,
This child will no longer be cast aside.

For I am the forgotten child,
I was forgotten only because
My mother was in chains
My father was bound
And I was without love.

[def-uh-nish-uh n]

It is love that will save us three, It is love that will set us free
No more chains to weigh us down, No more ropes to keep us bound.

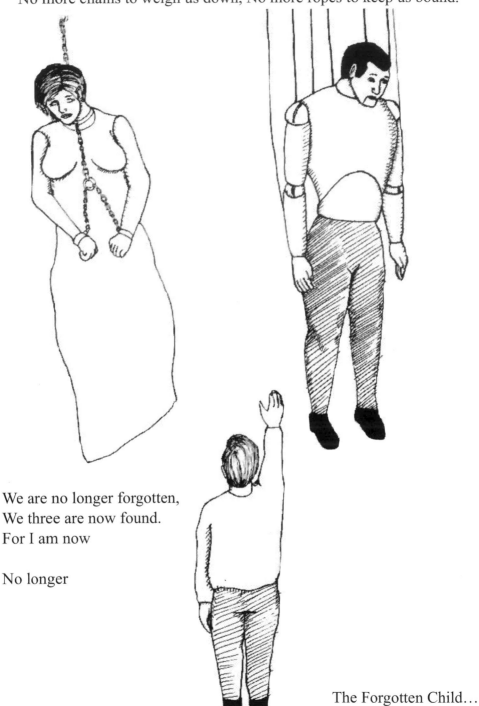

We are no longer forgotten,
We three are now found.
For I am now

No longer

The Forgotten Child…

[def-uh-nish-uh n]

Love Is

Opposing what "Fear Is", is to know what
"Love Is". Understanding, compassion,
patience, applying these virtues to life is to
know what love truly is. It is the absence of
fear in all degrees. Love is the definite in
life where fear is the indefinite indecision.

Love is what it is.

It just is…

-Outlaw G

[def-uh-nish-uh n]

Love Is

What opposes the light that is love?
Fear
Of what is not
Cannot be
Never was.
It is all because
Love does not dwell in iniquity
Fear does and embraces that complexity
Fear will be the death of all throughout eternity
Love is the breath that breathes life eternally.

Love is, Fear is not.

Love is the shield that protects
Fear is the disease that infects
Love is what reconnects
Fear is what redirects
Intercepts
Misrepresents and causes tension
Inflictions
Fear is what causes indecision
Love is precision.
Love understands
Fear over demands
When Fear says it can't
Love knows it can.
While Fear is insecure
Love remains pure
For pure love is true Love
Love always endures.

Love is, Fear is not.

[def-uh-nish-uh n]

Love is not lost or easily left behind
Even if Fear sends shivers down your spine
Love is eternal, it transcends space and time
It is the light of love that redefines and shines
Bright into the darkness
For Love is gentle and kind
It will always be there
To ease your heart and your mind.

Love is, Fear is not.

For Love is understanding
Comprehending
Allowing ears to hear
Fear takes that all away
Producing pain
Reducing you to tears
For Love is strength
Fear is weakness
Love conquers all
And allows you to speak this,
"I Love You."

Let these words ring true
And let the light of love
Forever guide you.
Love will be right beside you
Love won't lie to you.
Love is
Was
Love is forever, EternalE
Love is what Fear cannot be.

Love is…

[def-uh-nish-uh n]

Love's Lesson

People always ask the Who? What? When? Where? Why? and How? in regards to life. Most will ask these questions in regards to love. It is my hope to help you understand that these questions can all be answered by love, thus being the only real answer to these questions in life. It is "Love's Lesson" that will teach us that not all things need to be questioned, if they have already been answered.

-Outlaw G

[def-uh-nish-uh n]

Love's Lesson

Who defines Love?
I do, for no word spoken can be more true
The words "I Love You" are words I live and die for
If you Love me
I will Love you more.
I know love for I show love
I have the power to define it
I refine it
With a hug and a kiss
Also with the words "I miss"
For I miss you more.
It leaves me weak with shivers
That means love flows through me like a river,
I define it as something that keeps me floating back to you.

What is Love for?

Love comforts against the cold of life
A warm fire
A lit candle
Against the cold night.
It is for the broken and torn down
To be lifted and raised up from the ground
It is for those who feel empty
It is for those who feel simply
That life is not worth living.
Love is for all the beating hearts that miss those that aren't
Love is for the waiting hearts that need a spark
Love is for you and for me to keep us bound,
We can be lost in Love
And still be found.

[def-uh-nish-uh n]

When will Love find me?

Love is kind and always has time
For those who find themselves in an emotional bind
Love will be with you through life's unforgivable grind
And then it is when you will find
Love is not bound by time.
For it is
Was
And is forever
Leave you,
Never
Hurt you,
Never
For love is something better.
Love is always on time
Love's own time
So don't worry
It is not you Love has to find
It is you who has to open up your eyes.

Where is the Love?

Love has no barriers and has no walls
Love has no limits
Love encompasses all
Love conquers all.
A phrase that displays Love's true power
Love is in the air
It rains like showers
Love is the in flowers
That bloom in the spring
Love is in the birds
That perch and sing,
Out my window, bringing me the info of the day
Love is the sunshine that drives the pain away.

[def-uh-nish-uh n]

Love is where?
Love is here
Near
It is right beside you
Behind you
In front of you
It surrounds you
You just don't know it, yet.

Why Love?

Love is understanding and comprehension
When there is anger and tension
Love relieves the infliction
Love begins its own diction,
Its has its own language to be spoken and be heard
Love is more than just a four letter word
Love is more than ring with a rock
Love is more than a heart shaped box
Love creates life
Love defeats strife
Love is the reason to live
Love is the reason for life.
Love will never let you die
For memories and legacies live in eternity
Why Love?
Because Love
Loves EternalE.

How…. The final question to this lesson.

How does one Love?
Love is not difficult
Love isn't always something physical
Visual,
No
It goes deeper.

[def-uh-nish-uh n]

It's mental
Emotional
It is a soul seeker.
Love is the keeper
Of life and time
Love means what's mine is yours
And what's yours is mine.
Understand,
That love cannot be misunderstood
Love is not would,
Could,
Or should.
Love is can
Will
Love is definite
Love is unconditional,
Love bears no exceptions in it.
How does one Love?
They are absorbed in it
Molded by it
Live and die in it.
When you truly break it down
And you know Love to its core,
You will never ask how to Love anymore.

Here ends the lesson
Marked with this confession
That Love is absolute,
Love is not to be questioned.
This is Love's Lesson.

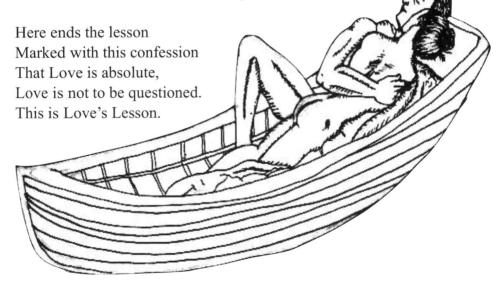

[def-uh-nish-uh n]

<u>EternalE</u>

In the constant battle between Love and Fear, we have to keep in mind both are eternal. Both fear and love can consume people but neither side can ever be vanquished. Fear is eternal, because it is our nature to fear what we don't understand, thus leading to anger and hate. Love is eternal because, as stated before, it is. This struggle between the two are eternal. It is ultimately our choice as rational or irrational human beings to Love or Fear, EternalE.

-Outlaw G

EternalE

What lies in infinity
Eternally
Worth everything
But costs nothing?

The word most heard
Never misunderstood
One word that could never hurt
That can turn evil, good.

One word that can make any man
Into something even better than
What he was the day before,
It does more than restore.

One word that can
Help every woman who can't,
Make it through another day
All you have to do is say,
"I love you."

When you say it, be true
With conviction
Speak with the diction
Of the the perfect definition
Of Love.

For it is Love
That will never let you fall to "The Bottom",
Instead, it will pull you up from every problem
For true love is due love and doesn't care what "Fear Is"
And true love will never ask this question,

[def-uh-nish-uh n]

"Why Are You So Messy?"
For happiness lies within the "Time Never Wasted"
Wrapped in love that allows you to face this
Life,
That "One Day" may try to take you away
Love keeps you Eternal
So your memory will never fade.

A "Liar" may try to bring you some pain
Leave you helpless like "The Woman in Chains"
Or leave you defenseless like the "The Bound Man"
Do not fret
For Love has a plan
To release you back into the wild
So you can find "The Forgotten Child"
Smile,
For you have come to understand
That "Love Is"
Love was
Love forever will be
Spell it out,
L
O
V
Ending with the eternal E
Thus eternally,
"Love's Lesson" rings free.

It is in the minds and the hearts that are open,
Focused on growing
Showing
Knowing what love truly is
More than a word to be heard
Love is the greatest,
Force in this life,
On the earth,
In existence.

[def-uh-nish-uh n]

Love is why we have existed,
For as long as we have for it is gifted
Passed down and passed on
Till the end of our days are gone.
Love lives on.

EternalE

[def-uh-nish-uh n]

[def-uh-nish-uh n]

Made in the USA
Columbia, SC
04 September 2021